SKIES OF DESTINY: ANALYZING THE INFLUENCE OF PLANETARY INTERPRETATIONS IN MEDIEVAL EUROPE AND ISLAMIC GOLDEN AGE

First edition. October 23, 2023.

Copyright © 2023 René Vermandois and R. Vermandois.

ISBN: 979-8223218814

Written by René Vermandois and R. Vermandois.

Table of Contents

Chapter 1: Introduction 1

Chapter 2: The Foundations of Astrology 7

Chapter 3: The Medieval European Astrological Practices 13

Chapter 4: The Islamic Astrological Traditions 19

Chapter 5: Cosmic Influences on Politics and Governance 25

Chapter 6: Astrology's Role in Medicine and Healing 31

Chapter 7: Astrology and Astronomy: Differentiating the Two 37

Chapter 8: The Influence of Planetary Interpretations on Art and Architecture 43

Chapter 9: Advanced Mathematical Methods in Astrology 49

Chapter 10: Celestial Navigation and Seafaring Explorations 55

Chapter 11: The Decline of Astrological Practices 61

Skies of Destiny: Analyzing the Influence of Planetary Interpretations in Medieval Europe and Islamic Golden Age

Chapter 1: Introduction

Setting the stage for the exploration of planetary interpretations, examining the significance of astrology and astronomy during the medieval period in Europe and the Islamic Golden Age.

The medieval period in Europe and the Islamic Golden Age were remarkable eras that shaped the course of history and left an indelible mark on scientific and intellectual development. Within these epochs, the study of planetary interpretations, astrology, and astronomy thrived, captivating the minds of scholars, philosophers, and theologians alike. In this chapter, we will embark on a journey to understand the profound influence of these celestial pursuits during these vibrant periods.

To grasp the significance of planetary interpretations in both medieval Europe and the Islamic Golden Age, it is essential to comprehend the prevailing beliefs and cultural contexts of the time. Throughout history, celestial bodies have held a special place in human civilizations, often believed to possess great power and influence over terrestrial affairs. The study of astrology, the art of interpreting the movements and positions of celestial bodies to predict and understand human events, was deeply intertwined with the socio-cultural fabric of these societies.

In medieval Europe, astrology was considered a vital tool for understanding the divine order of the universe. It was seen as a means of deciphering the will of God and discerning one's destiny. Kings and emperors relied on astrologers to guide them in decision-making, and even common people sought astrological advice to navigate their lives. The belief that the movement of the heavens reflected and affected earthly occurrences became deeply embedded in the medieval European psyche.

Simultaneously, the Islamic Golden Age witnessed a similar fascination with astrology and a flourishing of astronomical knowledge. Islamic scholars, deeply influenced by ancient Greek texts, dedicated themselves to advancing the study of astronomy as a means to uncover the purpose and structure of the universe. Drawing from their rich scientific heritage, they diligently observed the heavens, developed sophisticated astronomical instruments, and made significant contributions to astronomical knowledge.

One of the most prominent figures of the Islamic Golden Age was the Persian polymath, Abu Rayhan al-Biruni. He not only made significant astronomical observations but also wrote extensively on astrology, making connections between celestial phenomena and earthly events. Al-Biruni's works exemplify the fusion of astrology and astronomy during this period, showcasing the multifaceted nature of celestial studies.

Beyond the spiritual and intellectual realms, astrology and astronomy had practical applications in diverse fields such as agriculture, navigation, and medicine. Farmers relied on astrological predictions of favorable planting seasons, sailors used celestial navigation to traverse the seas, and physicians incorporated astrological principles in their diagnoses and treatments. The intertwined nature of astrology, astronomy, and various disciplines of daily life underscores the pervasive influence of planetary interpretations during these epochs.

Moreover, the study of planetary interpretations was not confined to isolated pockets in Europe and the Islamic world. Scholars from these regions engaged in a robust exchange of ideas, translating and sharing texts across linguistic and cultural boundaries. These intellectual interactions fostered a mutual enrichment of knowledge and allowed for the preservation and dissemination of ancient wisdom.

As we delve further into this exploration, it is important to acknowledge the complexity and diversity of opinions surrounding astrology and astronomy during the medieval period. While these disciplines were highly regarded, they also faced criticism from skeptics, religious authorities, and philosophers who questioned the validity and morality of relying on celestial interpretations. We will touch upon these debates and controversies, as they paint a comprehensive picture of the nuanced attitudes toward planetary interpretations.

In conclusion, this chapter has provided a glimpse into the rich tapestry of planetary interpretations during the medieval period in Europe and the Islamic Golden Age. We have seen how astrology and astronomy held a prominent place in the intellectual and cultural life of these societies, shaping beliefs, guiding decision-making, and influencing various facets of daily existence. However, to truly appreciate the extent and depth of this influence, we must further explore the key figures, texts, and scientific advancements that emerged during this vibrant era. In the following sections, we will delve deeper into the notable contributions and remarkable discoveries made in these diverse regions. Stay tuned for the second half of this chapter, where we will uncover the individuals and milestones that propelled planetary interpretations to new heights!In the second half of this chapter, we will continue our exploration of the significant figures, texts, and scientific advancements that propelled planetary interpretations to new heights during the medieval period in Europe and the Islamic Golden Age. These exceptional individuals and milestones not only expanded our knowledge of the heavens but also solidified the influence of astrology and astronomy on various domains.

In medieval Europe, one cannot overlook the contributions of Claudius Ptolemy, an influential Greek astronomer and geographer whose works had a lasting impact on celestial studies. Ptolemy's magnum opus, the Almagest, synthesized the astronomical knowledge of his time, providing a comprehensive treatise on the movements and positions of celestial bodies. His geocentric model, which placed the Earth at the center of the universe, dominated astronomical thought in Europe for over a millennium. Ptolemy's work not only laid the foundation for medieval European astrology and astronomy but also influenced Islamic scholars in their pursuits.

In the Islamic Golden Age, one of the most noteworthy figures in the field of planetary interpretations was the Persian polymath Al-Farabi. Known as "the Second Master" after Aristotle, Al-Farabi made significant contributions to both philosophy and the sciences. He explored the relationship between astrology and ethics, emphasizing the importance of studying the heavens to understand human behavior and guide individuals towards moral virtue. Al-Farabi's works, such as The Book of Letters, integrated philosophical and astrological ideas in a way that shaped Islamic thought and influenced later scholars.

Another prominent scholar during the Islamic Golden Age was the Persian mathematician and astronomer, Omar Khayyam. Although best known for his poetic masterpiece, the Rubaiyat, Khayyam also made substantial contributions to astronomy through his mathematical calculations of planetary motion. His work on algebraic solutions to geometric problems helped refine astronomical observations and advanced the study of planetary interpretations. Khayyam's combination of mathematical rigor with astronomical inquiry exemplified the interdisciplinary nature of celestial studies during this period.

While Ptolemy, Al-Farabi, and Khayyam were instrumental in shaping the theoretical understanding of celestial phenomena, the Islamic Golden Age also witnessed remarkable advancements in practical astronomy. The construction of precise astronomical instruments, such as the astrolabe and quadrant, allowed for accurate measurements and observations of the heavens. Islamic scholars, including Al-Battani and Al-Zarqali, made significant improvements to these instruments, enhancing their utility in celestial navigation and timekeeping. These developments not only facilitated transoceanic explorations but also had profound implications for trade, geography, and the expansion of knowledge.

In medieval Europe, a pivotal figure in advancing astronomical knowledge was Nicolaus Copernicus, whose comprehensive work, De Revolutionibus, challenged the prevailing geocentric model and instead proposed a heliocentric theory of the universe. Copernicus' revolutionary ideas not only laid the groundwork for modern astronomy but also sparked debates and controversies within the religious and intellectual spheres. His heliocentric model ultimately reshaped our understanding of planetary interpretations and the position of humans within the vast cosmos.

The multifaceted interactions between medieval Europe and the Islamic Golden Age played a crucial role in fostering the exchange and transmission of astronomical knowledge. The translation movement, initiated by Islamic scholars during the Abbasid Caliphate, facilitated the translation of ancient Greek and Persian texts into Arabic. These translated works, alongside the original contributions of Islamic scholars, then found their way into the Latin-speaking world of Europe, where they influenced and shaped the intellectual landscape. The interplay between these two civilizations not only preserved ancient wisdom but also propelled the study of planetary interpretations to new heights.

As we conclude this chapter, we have witnessed the profound influence of planetary interpretations in both medieval Europe and the Islamic Golden Age. From the belief that celestial bodies held significant power and influence over earthly events to the practical applications in various disciplines, astrology and astronomy permeated every aspect of life. The exceptional figures discussed in this chapter, like Ptolemy, Al-Farabi,

Khayyam, and Copernicus, served as pillars of knowledge, pushing the boundaries of understanding and challenging existing paradigms.

In the chapters to come, we will delve further into the intricacies of medieval Europe and the Islamic Golden Age, exploring additional figures, texts, and scientific advancements that continued to shape and expand our understanding of planetary interpretations. From the groundbreaking observations of Tycho Brahe and the mathematical precision of Johannes Kepler to the celestial mappings of Ulugh Beg and the astronomical instruments of Ibn Yunus, each contribution will weave together a comprehensive tapestry of celestial studies during these remarkable periods of history. Stay tuned as we unravel the wonders of the skies and uncover the stories behind the stars.

Chapter 2: The Foundations of Astrology

Astrology, an ancient practice that has captivated the minds of scholars and enthusiasts for centuries, has its roots deeply embedded in history. To truly understand its significance and evolution, we must embark on a journey back to the medieval times, where the foundations of astrology were laid. Exploring both the contexts of medieval Europe and the Islamic Golden Age, we peel back the layers of time, unveiling the historical origins of astrology and its intriguing development.

In medieval Europe, astrology emerged in a landscape influenced by Christianity and classical philosophy. The fusion of these two forces birthed a unique understanding of the cosmos, blending religious beliefs with intellectual pursuits. The medieval Christian scholars sought to reconcile pagan ideas with their religious principles, leading to a compelling interplay between divine theology and celestial observations.

The works of influential figures such as Claudius Ptolemy, a prominent Greek astronomer, played a pivotal role in shaping the understanding of astrology in medieval Europe. Ptolemy's magnum opus, the "Tetrabiblos," acted as a foundation for astrological teachings during this era. His meticulous observations and mathematical calculations presented a framework that resonated with medieval scholars, offering them a scientific basis for their astrological endeavors.

However, the study of astrology during this period was not confined solely to Europe. A parallel narrative unfolded in the Islamic Golden Age, where Muslim scholars embraced astrology as a means to decipher God's divine plan. The Islamic civilization, known for its pursuit of knowledge across various disciplines, fostered a rich astrological tradition that influenced both the Eastern and Western worlds.

Islamic astronomers, such as Al-Farabi and Al-Kindi, significantly contributed to the development of astrology during this era. Drawing from their extensive knowledge of mathematics and astronomy, they expanded upon the foundations laid by Ptolemy and other classical scholars. Their works not only advanced astrological techniques but also explored the philosophical implications of celestial influences on human affairs.

Astrology, in both medieval Europe and the Islamic Golden Age, served as a tool for understanding and predicting the interconnectedness between celestial bodies and earthly events. It was believed that the positions and movements of planets, stars, and constellations held profound significance, influencing the lives of individuals and the fate of nations. By unraveling the mysteries of the heavens, astrologers sought to gain insight into human destinies and societal transformations.

Additionally, astrology played a pivotal role in medieval medicine. Physicians and healers regarded it as an essential part of their diagnostic and therapeutic practices. The belief in the interplay between the human body and the celestial realm led to the development of astrological medicine, wherein treatments and remedies were tailored according to planetary alignments and astrological charts.

As astrology flourished in both medieval Europe and the Islamic Golden Age, it wove itself into the very fabric of society. Kings and queens consulted astrologers to guide their decisions, while common people sought solace in astrological predictions. Astrologers adorned the courts of emperors, and scholars debated the intricate frameworks of astrology in the hallowed halls of academia.

The foundations set during this time paved the way for astrology's enduring impact on subsequent centuries. Its influence permeated literature, art, and even navigational practices. The echoes of medieval astrology can be heard in the works of renowned authors like Geoffrey Chaucer and Dante Alighieri, where celestial motifs and astrological symbolism abound.

The first half of our exploration into the foundations of astrology concludes here, leaving us on the cusp of a grand revelation. We have journeyed through time, witnessing the convergence of religious beliefs, philosophical musings, and celestial observations. The next part of this chapter will delve deeper into the intricate practices and developments that shaped astrology in medieval Europe and the Islamic Golden Age.

With anticipation and the thrill of discovery, we move forward, ready to unravel the complexities of this ancient art and its enduring allure. Join us as we navigate the depths of medieval astrological traditions, unearthing the mysteries and unveiling the hidden connections between the heavens and humanity.

In the magnificent tapestry of history, astrology emerges as a vibrant thread that weaves together the celestial realm with the affairs of humanity. As we continue our journey through the foundations of astrology in medieval Europe and the Islamic Golden Age, we dive deeper into the intricate practices and developments that shaped this ancient art.

In medieval Europe, astrology found firm footing within the realm of medicine. Physicians and healers believed in the connection between the human body and the celestial forces, and thus turned to astrological principles for guidance in their diagnostic and therapeutic endeavors. Known as astrological medicine, this approach involved tailoring treatments and remedies according to planetary alignments and astrological charts. The belief was that the positions and movements of celestial bodies could influence the course of diseases and the effectiveness of treatments.

Astrological medicine reached its zenith during the Middle Ages, particularly in the Islamic Golden Age. The Islamic civilization was known for its profound contributions to various fields of knowledge, and astrology was no exception. Muslim scholars recognized the potential of astrology in medical practices and emphasized the importance of aligning treatments with planetary configurations. Influential figures such as Ibn Sina, famously known as Avicenna, expanded upon the works of earlier scholars and developed comprehensive medical astrology systems.

Avicenna's "The Canon of Medicine" revolutionized medical practices in the Islamic world and beyond. This seminal work integrated astrology into the diagnosis and treatment of diseases, emphasizing the influence of celestial bodies on bodily humors and the overall well-being of individuals. The principles outlined in "The Canon" provided a framework for physicians to consider the astrological influences when prescribing remedies and performing healing rituals.

Apart from the medical realm, astrology also permeated the daily lives of individuals during this era. Astrologers were consulted for a myriad of purposes, ranging from determining auspicious dates for significant events to guiding personal choices. Kings and queens relied on astrologers to make strategic decisions, believing that the alignment of the stars could tip the scales of fortune in their favor. Even the common people sought solace and guidance from astrological predictions, seeking to navigate the uncertainties of life through the wisdom of the heavens.

The impact of astrology extended beyond individual lives and intermingled with cultures, literature, and art. Celestial motifs and astrological symbolism found their way into the works of renowned authors like Geoffrey Chaucer and Dante Alighieri, enriching their literary masterpieces. In Chaucer's "The Canterbury Tales," for example, astrology forms an essential backdrop to the stories, illustrating the pervasive influence of astrological beliefs in medieval society.

As astrology flourished during this period, it also played a vital role in navigation. Sailors and explorers of the time ventured into uncharted waters, relying on celestial observations to navigate their way through the vast oceans. Astrological charts and instruments, such as astrolabes, provided crucial guidance by mapping the positions of stars and planets, ensuring safe and successful voyages of discovery.

The enduring fascination with astrology in medieval Europe and the Islamic Golden Age shaped not only cultural aspects but also scientific pursuits. Scholars engaged in debates and discussions, seeking to comprehend the complexities and implications of astrology alongside advancements in other fields such as mathematics and astronomy.

The study of astrology in medieval Europe and the Islamic Golden Age was far from one-dimensional. It encompassed a blend of mathematical calculations, theological considerations, and philosophical musings. Astrologers, scholars, and enthusiasts contended with questions of fate, free will, and the nature of the cosmos, debating the intricate frameworks of astrology in the hallowed halls of academia.

As our exploration into the foundations of astrology in medieval Europe and the Islamic Golden Age draws to a close, we come to appreciate the vastness of its influence throughout history. The intricate practices and developments we have uncovered provide glimpses into a time where celestial observations and divine musings interconnected, shaping the way societies perceived their place within the cosmos.

These foundations paved the way for the enduring allure of astrology in subsequent centuries, where its echoes resound in the works of astronomers, philosophers, and theologians. From the realms of medicine to art, literature, and navigation, astrology left an indelible mark on history, merging the heavens with humanity in an eternal dance.

As we bid farewell to this chapter, we embark on the following chapters of our journey, where we will delve into the profound impact of astrology on specific areas such as medicine, philosophy, and politics. Join us as we further unveil the mysteries and hidden connections between the skies of destiny and the intricate tapestry of human existence.

Chapter 3: The Medieval European Astrological Practices

The skies have always held a mysterious allure for humankind. From ancient civilizations to modern societies, humans have gazed at the celestial bodies in search of meaning, guidance, and a deeper understanding of the world around them. In medieval Europe, the practice of astrology flourished, deeply ingrained in the religious beliefs and societal structures of the time. This chapter delves into an in-depth exploration of the astrological practices prevalent in medieval Europe, unraveling the intricate connections between astrology, religion, and society.

To comprehend the significance of astrology in medieval Europe, one must first grasp the prevalent mindset and worldview of the time. The European medieval period was characterized by a deeply religious atmosphere, with Christianity dominating both spiritual and secular aspects of life. Within this framework, astrology emerged as a vital tool to interpret the divine plan and to better understand the individual's place within the cosmic order.

Astrology held the belief that the positions and movements of celestial bodies, such as the Sun, Moon, planets, and stars, had a profound impact on the events transpiring on Earth. This belief formed the foundation of astrological practices in medieval Europe, where scholars and practitioners meticulously studied celestial configurations to discern certain patterns and predict future outcomes. Such practices relied on extensive astronomical observations, mathematical calculations, and the formulation of complex astrological charts.

The Church, despite its central role in medieval European society, held a complex relationship with astrology. While the Church officially condemned divinatory practices, including astrology, as superstitious and potentially heretical, astrology managed to find its place within the clergy. Many clergymen possessed a deep understanding of astrology and actively engaged in its study, often seeking to harmonize it with Christian theology.

Astrology became particularly influential in matters of medicine, as practitioners believed that the celestial bodies held sway over the human body and its processes. The concept of "medical astrology" gained prominence, with physicians using astrological charts to diagnose diseases, prescribe treatments, and determine the timing of medical interventions. Astrological associations with the zodiac signs and the planets were integrated into medical texts, contributing to the development of astrological medicine throughout medieval Europe.

Moreover, astrology's influence extended beyond the realm of health and wellness. Kings, nobles, and prominent figures sought astrologers' counsel for guidance on political matters, military campaigns, and matters of governance. Astrologers were often called upon to interpret celestial signs and predict the success or failure of certain endeavors, offering invaluable advice to rulers seeking to solidify their power and maintain the stability of their realms.

Society at large recognized the authority of astrologers, acknowledging their role as intermediaries between the divine and human realms. Astrologers held a position of respect and prominence, with their predictions and interpretations shaping the decisions and actions of individuals and communities alike. Furthermore, the influence of astrology seeped into the daily lives of the general population, as horoscopes and astrological forecasts became a common part of popular culture.

As societal structures and religious beliefs shifted throughout medieval Europe, astrology remained a constant force, adapting to changing circumstances while maintaining its influential presence. The interplay between religion, society, and astrology created a dynamic landscape where the practice thrived, despite occasional condemnation from religious authorities.

In the second part of this chapter, we will delve deeper into the specific astrological practices prevalent in different regions of medieval Europe. We will explore the contributions of notable scholars and astrologers, unravel the intricacies of astrological charts, and analyze the impact of astrology on the lives of individuals and the broader societal framework. Join us as we navigate through the celestial realms, unraveling the secrets of medieval European astrological practices.

The specific astrological practices prevalent in different regions of medieval Europe varied, reflecting the diverse cultural and intellectual landscapes of the time. This second half of the chapter will explore the contributions of notable scholars and astrologers, unravel the intricacies of astrological charts, and analyze the impact of astrology on the lives of individuals and the broader societal framework.

One region where astrology thrived was the Iberian Peninsula, particularly under the influence of Islamic rule during the Islamic Golden Age. Muslim astronomers and astrologers made significant advancements in the field, translating and expanding upon the astronomical works of ancient civilizations such as the Greeks and Persians. Figures like Al-Zarqali (also known as Azarquiel) in Moorish Spain and Al-Biruni in the Islamic world played a crucial role in promoting astrology and its integration with Islamic and Christian religious beliefs.

In Western Europe, the practice of astrology was deeply intertwined with alchemy, which sought to uncover the secrets of transmuting base metals into gold and achieving immortality. Alchemists believed that the celestial bodies exerted powerful influences on the physical world and human existence. Astrologers, skilled in the interpretation of celestial movements, were consulted for their expertise in determining propitious times for alchemical experiments and endeavors.

The Renaissance period witnessed an increased fascination with astrology, driven by a quest for knowledge and the rediscovery of classical works. Influential figures such as Niccolo Machiavelli and Leonardo da Vinci were known to consult astrologers for guidance. Alongside the newfound popularity of astrology, critics also emerged. Prominent humanists like Marsilio Ficino sought to reconcile astrology with Christian beliefs, while others, like the reformer Martin Luther, denounced it as a form of paganism.

Astrological charts, known as birth charts or horoscopes, were an essential tool in the practice. These charts depicted the positions of the celestial bodies at the time of an individual's birth and served as a framework for interpreting their personality traits, life events, and potential future outcomes. Astrologers analyzed each component of the chart, including the zodiac signs, planets, and their aspects, to provide insights into various aspects of the individual's life.

The impact of astrology extended beyond personal lives and permeated political and military decision-making. Rulers frequently sought the guidance of astrologers to ascertain the most auspicious times for coronations, the commencement of battles, or the negotiation of treaties. The interpretation of celestial signs played a vital role in strategic planning, ensuring that rulers aligned their actions with the perceived cosmic order and avoided potential disasters.

Astrology also had a profound influence on the architecture and layout of cities in medieval Europe. The concept of "astrological urbanism" emerged, which involved the design of urban spaces in accordance with astrological principles. The positioning of streets, buildings, and structures was guided by astrological considerations, such as the alignment of important landmarks with significant celestial events or zodiacal signs. This approach aimed to harness the supposed cosmic energies for the benefit and harmony of the city's inhabitants.

However, despite its widespread acceptance and influence in medieval society, astrology faced occasional backlash from religious authorities. The Church's condemnation of divinatory practices extended to astrology, viewing it as a potential threat to Christian teachings and asserting that it undermined human free will and the pivotal role of divine intervention. Yet, even in the face of official censure, astrology persisted, adapting to changing circumstances and retaining its sway over the minds of individuals.

In conclusion, astrology held a prominent position in medieval European society, deeply connected to religious beliefs, societal structures, and intellectual pursuits. From the Iberian Peninsula to Western Europe and the Renaissance period, astrology evolved and merged with various cultural and scientific practices, leaving a lasting impact on the lives of individuals and the broader fabric of society. It both reflected and shaped the worldviews of its practitioners and remains an intriguing lens through which to explore the multifaceted medieval European identity.

Chapter 4: The Islamic Astrological Traditions

Delving into the rich Islamic astrological traditions, their mathematical foundations, and the influence of Persian and Indian astrological techniques, we uncover a world of celestial exploration that spans across centuries and continents. Islamic astrological traditions developed during the Islamic Golden Age, a time of flourishing intellectual and cultural exchange between the Islamic world and various civilizations, particularly in Medieval Europe.

During this era, Islamic scholars made significant advancements in the field of astrology, building upon the knowledge and techniques inherited from ancient Persia and India. These scholars recognized the importance of studying the movements of the heavens and mapping the celestial bodies for both practical and metaphysical purposes. Thus, they began to meticulously observe the stars, planets, and constellations, seeking to unlock the mysteries of the universe.

In order to understand the foundations of Islamic astrology, we must first examine the mathematical principles that underpin this ancient art. Islamic astronomers developed intricate mathematical models to calculate the positions and movements of the celestial bodies with remarkable accuracy. They refined the works of ancient Greek astronomers like Ptolemy and Hipparchus, incorporating their knowledge into their own cosmological theories.

One of the prominent figures in the Islamic astrological tradition is Al-Kindi, an influential philosopher and polymath. Al-Kindi emphasized the importance of mathematical precision in astrology, arguing that accurate calculations were essential to interpreting celestial phenomena. He sought to refine the existing mathematical models, making them more compatible with Islamic theological doctrines and the Arabic numerical system.

Another notable contributor to Islamic astrology was Abu Ma'shar al-Balkhi, commonly known as Albumasar. This Persian astrologer played a crucial role in disseminating astrological knowledge throughout the Islamic world. Albumasar's works, such as the "Book of Flowers," explored various astrological techniques and their applications. He drew insights from both ancient Greek and Indian astrological traditions, aiming to cultivate a comprehensive and holistic approach to the subject.

The influence of Persian and Indian astrological techniques cannot be understated when examining Islamic astrology. Persian astrologers, such as Balinus and Al-Farghani, made significant contributions to the field, particularly in the domains of astronomy and astrological predictions. The Persian influence can be seen in the prominence given to the fixed stars, their constellations, and their corresponding interpretations.

Similarly, Indian astrological concepts and techniques made their way into Islamic astrology, enriching the field with a diverse array of ideas. The Indian concept of the "navagrahas," or nine planets, greatly influenced Islamic astrological theories. These nine celestial bodies, including the Sun, Moon, Mars, Mercury, Jupiter, Venus, Saturn, Rāhu, and Ketu, were believed to wield immense influence over human lives, affecting everything from personality traits to fortune and misfortune.

As Islamic astrologers absorbed and integrated these diverse influences, they developed their own unique interpretations and practices. Astrological predictions, horoscope readings, and the casting of charts became integral parts of the Islamic cultural landscape, providing insights into the past, present, and future. The meticulous observations and calculations made by Islamic astrologers not only fascinated the scholarly elite but also captivated the imagination of the general public, fostering a widespread interest and belief in astrological phenomena.

In conclusion, the Islamic astrological traditions emerged during the Islamic Golden Age, where scholars built upon the foundations laid by ancient Persia and India. Through the refinement of mathematical models, the works of great thinkers like Al-Kindi and Albumasar, and the incorporation of Persian and Indian techniques, Islamic astrology came to flourish. The meticulous observations and calculations made by Islamic astrologers paved the way for a deeper understanding of the universe and its influence on human lives. The rich Islamic astrological traditions continue to inspire and intrigue history and geography readers to this day...The development of Islamic astrological traditions during the Islamic Golden Age was not limited to the refinement of mathematical models and the incorporation of Persian and Indian techniques. It also involved the exploration of the metaphysical aspects of astrology and the belief in celestial influences on human lives.

Islamic scholars recognized the interconnectedness between the celestial bodies and the earthly realm. They believed that the positions and movements of the stars and planets exerted a profound influence on human destiny. This understanding led to the popularization of horoscope readings and astrological predictions as tools for exploring one's past, understanding the present, and foreseeing the future.

Astrological predictions played a significant role in various aspects of Islamic society. They were consulted before important events, such as the coronation of a ruler, the signing of treaties, or the beginning of major military campaigns. Islamic astrologers would cast charts and analyze the planetary positions at the time of these significant events to offer guidance and insight into their outcomes.

Astrology also provided a means for understanding personal characteristics, compatibility, and potential outcomes for individuals.

Islamic scholars developed detailed horoscope readings, known as "tajwa'ids," which provided comprehensive analyses of an individual's personality, strengths, weaknesses, and potential paths in life. These readings were often sought by individuals seeking guidance in matters of love, career, and personal growth.

One notable aspect of Islamic astrological traditions was the interpretation of celestial phenomena as divine signs or omens. Islamic scholars believed that the movements and alignments of the celestial bodies held symbolic meanings, indicating possible events and outcomes in the physical and spiritual realms. These interpretations were deeply rooted in religious and spiritual beliefs, contributing to the integration of astrology into Islamic culture.

Astrological symbolism and interpretations were not confined to the Islamic world alone. They also influenced the development of astrology in Medieval Europe. During the Islamic Golden Age, the Islamic astrological traditions made their way to Europe through translations of Arabic texts. These European scholars, intrigued by the rich Muslim heritage of celestial exploration, sought to incorporate Islamic astrological knowledge into their own practices.

The cultural exchange between the Islamic world and Medieval Europe facilitated a blending of astrological traditions and techniques. European scholars, such as Roger Bacon and Gerard of Cremona, drew upon Islamic astrological manuscripts, incorporating them into their own works. This infusion of Islamic astrological knowledge played a crucial role in shaping the European Renaissance and the subsequent development of astrology in Western societies.

The legacy of Islamic astrological traditions can still be seen in various aspects of contemporary astrology. The use of Arabic terms, the influence of Islamic mathematical models, and the inclusion of Persian and Indian astrological techniques continue to influence astrological practices today. Astrologers and scholars alike study the contributions of Islamic thinkers and incorporate their insights into modern interpretations and applications of astrology.

In conclusion, the Islamic astrological traditions of the Islamic Golden Age spanned centuries and continents, encompassing a blend of mathematical precision, metaphysical beliefs, and cultural exchanges. Islamic astrologers refined mathematical models, integrated Persian and Indian techniques, and sought to unlock the mysteries of the universe. The influence of Islamic astrology extended beyond the Islamic world, shaping astrological practices in Medieval Europe and continuing to inspire and inform contemporary astrology. The rich Islamic astrological traditions remain a testament to the intellectual and cultural achievements of the Islamic Golden Age.

Chapter 5: Cosmic Influences on Politics and Governance

Throughout history, political decisions, royal lineage claims, and the governance structures of societies have been shaped by various factors. One such factor, often overlooked but undeniably important, is the influence of astrological interpretations. In medieval Europe and the Islamic Golden Age, the belief in the link between celestial bodies and earthly affairs was widespread, leading to significant consequences in politics and governance.

To comprehend the extent of astrological influence on politics and governance during this time, one must first understand the prevailing astrological beliefs. Astrology, derived from the Greek word "astrologia," meaning "the study of stars," was a prominent discipline that sought to interpret the positions and movements of celestial bodies to understand their influence on human affairs. Medieval Europe and the Islamic Golden Age both witnessed a flourishing of astrological theories and practices, intertwined with religious and intellectual beliefs.

In medieval Europe, astrological interpretations served as a guiding tool in political decision-making. Rulers and nobility often consulted astrologers to determine the most auspicious times for important events, such as coronations, marriages, and even battles. Astrologers were seen as advisors who possessed a unique knowledge of the cosmos, able to predict celestial alignments that would portend success or failure. Their counsel held sway over rulers, influencing not only their personal decisions but also the fate of nations.

The close association between astrology and politics was particularly evident in matters of royal lineage claims. In an era where the legitimacy of rulers was closely tied to divine right, astrological interpretations were employed to validate hereditary claims. Astrologers were tasked with analyzing the birth charts of monarchs, searching for celestial signs of auspiciousness that would affirm their right to rule. Conversely, any unfavorable planetary alignments could be used to challenge a ruler's legitimacy or predict their downfall.

The Islamic Golden Age, on the other hand, witnessed a rich fusion of Islamic theology and astrology. Islamic scholars found inspiration in ancient Babylonian and Greek astrological texts, synthesizing them with Arab and Persian traditions. Astrology became an integral part of scientific inquiry and religious discourse. In the Islamic world, rulers and scholars alike utilized astrology as a means to understand and contemplate their place in the grand cosmic design.

The influence of astrological interpretations was not limited to individual rulers. Governance structures in both medieval Europe and the Islamic Golden Age were often founded on astrological principles. The aim was to align the governance of earthly realms with the celestial harmony believed to govern the universe. Concepts such as the "body politic" and the "Great Chain of Being" were employed to justify hierarchical structures, with rulers seen as instruments of divine will, acting in accordance with the cosmic order.

Astrological consultations were also sought to ensure the longevity and success of nations. Cities, as microcosms of the broader political landscape, were founded under auspicious astrological configurations. It was believed that by choosing the right celestial moment, a ruler could establish a harmonious and prosperous city. Similarly, the astrology of a nation's inception was scrutinized, as it was believed to offer insights into its destiny and future.

As we delve deeper into the influence of astrological interpretations on politics and governance, it becomes apparent that the belief in cosmic forces shaped the decision-making processes, royal claims, and foundational structures of societies in medieval Europe and the Islamic Golden Age. The interplay between the celestial and the earthly allowed rulers to assert their authority, legitimize their lineage, and establish governance structures that aimed to mirror the harmony of the universe.

However, it is vital to acknowledge the limitations and criticisms of astrological interpretations as well. Skeptics argue that relying on celestial alignments is mere pseudoscience, dismissive of rational thought and empirical evidence. Furthermore, the questions surrounding the universality and objectivity of astrological interpretations persist. Yet, regardless of debates surrounding its validity, astrology undeniably held significant sway over the political and governance spheres of medieval Europe and the Islamic Golden Age.

Thus astrology played a crucial role in shaping politics and governance during the medieval period in Europe and the Islamic Golden Age. The consultation of astrological interpretations in political decision-making, the validation of royal lineage claims, and the alignment of governance structures with the celestial order all bear witness to the profound and lasting influence of astrological beliefs. As we continue our exploration of cosmic influences on politics and governance, we shall uncover further intricacies and intriguing elements that will shed even more light on this captivating subject.

Throughout history, political decisions, royal lineage claims, and the governance structures of societies have been shaped by various factors. One such factor, often overlooked but undeniably important, is the influence of astrological interpretations. In medieval Europe and the Islamic Golden Age, the belief in the link between celestial bodies and earthly affairs was widespread, leading to significant consequences in politics and governance.

To comprehend the extent of astrological influence on politics and governance during this time, one must first understand the prevailing astrological beliefs. Astrology, derived from the Greek word "astrologia," meaning "the study of stars," was a prominent discipline that sought to interpret the positions and movements of celestial bodies to understand their influence on human affairs. Medieval Europe and the Islamic Golden Age both witnessed a flourishing of astrological theories and practices, intertwined with religious and intellectual beliefs.

In medieval Europe, astrological interpretations served as a guiding tool in political decision-making. Rulers and nobility often consulted astrologers to determine the most auspicious times for important events, such as coronations, marriages, and even battles. Astrologers were seen as advisors who possessed a unique knowledge of the cosmos, able to predict celestial alignments that would portend success or failure. Their counsel held sway over rulers, influencing not only their personal decisions but also the fate of nations.

The close association between astrology and politics was particularly evident in matters of royal lineage claims. In an era where the legitimacy of rulers was closely tied to divine right, astrological interpretations were employed to validate hereditary claims. Astrologers were tasked with analyzing the birth charts of monarchs, searching for celestial signs of auspiciousness that would affirm their right to rule. Conversely, any unfavorable planetary alignments could be used to challenge a ruler's legitimacy or predict their downfall.

The Islamic Golden Age, on the other hand, witnessed a rich fusion of Islamic theology and astrology. Islamic scholars found inspiration in ancient Babylonian and Greek astrological texts, synthesizing them with Arab and Persian traditions. Astrology became an integral part of scientific inquiry and religious discourse. In the Islamic world, rulers and scholars alike utilized astrology as a means to understand and contemplate their place in the grand cosmic design.

The influence of astrological interpretations was not limited to individual rulers. Governance structures in both medieval Europe and the Islamic Golden Age were often founded on astrological principles. The aim was to align the governance of earthly realms with the celestial harmony believed to govern the universe. Concepts such as the "body politic" and the "Great Chain of Being" were employed to justify hierarchical structures, with rulers seen as instruments of divine will, acting in accordance with the cosmic order.

Astrological consultations were also sought to ensure the longevity and success of nations. Cities, as microcosms of the broader political landscape, were founded under auspicious astrological configurations. It was believed that by choosing the right celestial moment, a ruler could establish a harmonious and prosperous city. Similarly, the astrology of a nation's inception was scrutinized, as it was believed to offer insights into its destiny and future.

As we delve deeper into the influence of astrological interpretations on politics and governance, it becomes apparent that the belief in cosmic forces shaped the decision-making processes, royal claims, and foundational structures of societies in medieval Europe and the Islamic Golden Age. The interplay between the celestial and the earthly allowed rulers to assert their authority, legitimize their lineage, and establish governance structures that aimed to mirror the harmony of the universe.

However, it is vital to acknowledge the limitations and criticisms of astrological interpretations as well. Skeptics argue that relying on celestial alignments is mere pseudoscience, dismissive of rational thought and empirical evidence. Furthermore, the questions surrounding the universality and objectivity of astrological interpretations persist. Yet, regardless of debates surrounding its validity, astrology undeniably held significant sway over the political and governance spheres of medieval Europe and the Islamic Golden Age.

In conclusion, astrology played a crucial role in shaping politics and governance during the medieval period in Europe and the Islamic Golden Age. The consultation of astrological interpretations in political decision-making, the validation of royal lineage claims, and the alignment of governance structures with the celestial order all bear witness to the profound and lasting influence of astrological beliefs.

The integration of celestial influences with political and governance systems highlights the complexity and depth of medieval societies. By considering the interplay of religious, intellectual, and astrological beliefs, historians and scholars gain a more nuanced understanding of how societies grappled with questions of power, legitimacy, and divine intervention.

The impact of astrological interpretations on politics and governance during the medieval period underscores the significance of cultural and intellectual contexts in shaping the course of history. By analyzing the enduring influence of celestial beliefs, we enrich our understanding of how medieval societies navigated the complexities of power, royal lineage, and governance, making decisions that were influenced by cosmic forces beyond their control.

As history and geography readers, we continue to explore and unravel the fascinating interconnections between celestial influences and political governance during the medieval period. By delving into the intricacies of astrological interpretations, we gain insights that shed light on the multifaceted nature of human civilizations and their eternal quest for meaning and order in the skies above.

Chapter 6: Astrology's Role in Medicine and Healing

Throughout the medieval period in Europe and the Islamic Golden Age, astrology played a significant role in shaping medical practices and beliefs. The integration of astrology into medicine had a profound impact on healthcare, influencing the understanding of diseases, treatment methods, and even patient perspectives. This chapter delves into the intriguing connection between astrology and medicine during medieval times, uncovering the ways in which celestial interpretations influenced healing practices.

In medieval Europe and the Islamic Golden Age, the prevailing belief was that celestial bodies, specifically the planets, held immense influence over human health and well-being. Astrology, the study of celestial movements and their impact on human affairs, provided a framework for understanding this connection. Physicians and healers of the time looked to astrology as a guiding tool in diagnosing illnesses, prescribing treatments, and predicting the course of diseases.

At the core of astrology's integration into medicine was the belief in the interconnectedness of the macrocosm (the universe) and the microcosm (the human body). Ancient texts such as Claudius Ptolemy's "Tetrabiblos" and Abu Ma'shar's "Great Introduction" served as primary sources for astrological principles in medicine. These texts emphasized the notion that each planet corresponded to a specific bodily organ or system. For instance, the sun was associated with the heart, the moon with the brain, and Saturn with the spleen. By understanding the positioning of these celestial bodies at the time of a person's birth, physicians believed they could determine potential health vulnerabilities or imbalances.

Astrological charts, known as horoscopes, became essential tools for medical practitioners. These charts mapped the precise positions of celestial bodies at the moment of a patient's birth, providing valuable insights into their predispositions and potential health issues. Physicians used this information to tailor treatments and prevention strategies accordingly. For example, if a person's astrological chart indicated a weak sun, practitioners might prescribe herbal remedies or practices aimed at strengthening the heart. Astrology thus informed both preventive and curative approaches to healthcare.

Additionally, astrology influenced medical treatments through its association with the humoral theory. According to this theory, the human body contained four principal fluids or humors: blood, phlegm, yellow bile, and black bile. Each humor was connected to a particular element and different planetary influences. By balancing these humors, physicians believed they could restore health. For instance, if an individual had an excess of yellow bile, associated with the element of fire and the planet Mars, treatments might involve cooling remedies or herbs ruled by the moon or Venus.

Astrology not only guided medical practitioners in their diagnosis and treatment decisions but also impacted patient perspectives on illness. People of the medieval period often sought medical advice based on their astrological charts, believing that their destiny was written in the stars. This outlook created a sense of reassurance and trust in the healing process, as patients felt that their condition was understood on a deeper, cosmic level. The integration of astrology into medicine provided a sense of structure and meaning, helping individuals cope with their ailments.

Moreover, astrology shaped the way diseases were understood and perceived. Astrological principles attributed certain illnesses to specific planetary alignments or imbalances. Physicians would consult astrological charts to identify the planetary influences contributing to an individual's illness. For instance, a person suffering from a skin condition might have an astrological alignment indicating affliction by Saturn, who was associated with dryness and diseases of the skin. This astrological insight informed the choice of treatments and remedies employed by physicians.

The integration of astrology into medicine during medieval times had far-reaching consequences on healthcare practices and beliefs. From diagnosing illnesses based on astrological charts to using planetary associations to navigate treatment decisions, astrology played a prominent role. Moreover, this intertwining of celestial interpretations with medicine influenced patient perspectives on illness, providing a sense of meaning and reassurance in times of vulnerability.

As we delve further into the realms of astrology's impact on medicine and healing, in the second half of this chapter, we will explore the influential figures who championed this integration, the diverse treatment methods employed, and delve into the controversies that surrounded the use of astrology within the medical community. Join us as we unravel the intricacies of this entwined relationship, and shed light on the enduring legacy of astrology's role in healthcare during medieval times. In the second half of this chapter, we will explore the influential figures who championed the integration of astrology into medicine during medieval times. These individuals played a pivotal role in advocating for the use of celestial interpretations in healthcare and further contributed to the development and refinement of medical practices.

One of the key figures in astrology's role in medicine was Ibn Sina, also known as Avicenna, an influential Persian philosopher and physician. Ibn Sina's masterpiece, "The Canon of Medicine," became a central text in the field of medicine and was heavily influenced by astrological principles. In his work, Ibn Sina emphasized the importance of considering celestial influences in the diagnosis and treatment of diseases. He believed that the positions and movements of the celestial bodies could both reflect and influence the state of the human body.

Another prominent figure in the integration of astrology and medicine was Gerard of Cremona, a translator and scholar who played a crucial role in translating and disseminating Arabic texts in Europe during the 12th century. Gerard's translations of works by renowned Arab physicians, including Ibn Sina, contributed to the spread of astrological knowledge and its incorporation into European medical practices. His efforts facilitated the transfer of medical knowledge between different cultures and significantly influenced the development of medical astrology in Europe.

Astrological treatments during medieval times encompassed a wide range of methods and practices. Herbal remedies, for example, were often prescribed based on astrological associations. Certain herbs were believed to be under the influence of specific planets, and their usage depended on the position of the planets in a patient's astrological chart. Physicians would carefully select herbs aligned with the celestial influences affecting the patient's health, aiming to restore balance and alleviate symptoms. These herbal treatments were commonly used for various ailments, such as digestive disorders, respiratory issues, and even mental health conditions.

In addition to herbal remedies, astrological medicine also involved bloodletting, a practice that aimed to balance the humors within the body. Bloodletting was performed based on the position of the moon, which was believed to influence blood circulation. Physicians would time bloodletting procedures according to specific astrological alignments to optimize their efficacy. While this practice may seem unconventional or even harmful by today's standards, it was an integral part of medical treatments during medieval times and exemplifies the extent to which astrology influenced medical practices.

However, the integration of astrology into medicine was not without controversy. Critics argued that medical decisions based on astrological charts lacked scientific rigor and were merely based on superstition. The medical community was divided, with some physicians embracing the use of astrology and others dismissing it entirely. Nonetheless, astrology's role in medicine persisted, predominantly due to its widespread acceptance among patients and their belief in the power of celestial influences.

Throughout the medieval period, astrology provided structure and meaning to both physicians and patients. The belief in the interconnectedness of the macrocosm and the microcosm fostered a sense of unity between celestial bodies and human health. Astrology served as a guiding tool for medical practitioners, shaping their understanding of diseases and treatments. It also provided patients with a sense of reassurance and understanding, as their ailments were perceived to be part of a larger cosmic pattern.

In conclusion, the integration of astrology into medicine during medieval times had a profound impact on healthcare practices and beliefs. Influential figures such as Ibn Sina and Gerard of Cremona championed the use of celestial interpretations in medicine, leading to the development of new treatment methods and the refinement of existing ones. Astrological principles guided medical practitioners in their diagnosis and treatment decisions, and herbal remedies and bloodletting were prescribed based on astrological associations. Despite controversy and divided opinions within the medical community, astrology remained an influential force in healthcare, providing structure, meaning, and a sense of cosmic connection for both physicians and patients.

As we conclude our exploration of the role of astrology in medicine and healing during medieval times, we have shed light on the enduring legacy of this intertwined relationship. By understanding the historical context and the influential individuals who shaped these practices, we gain valuable insight into the rich tapestry of beliefs and treatments that defined healthcare during this period. Through the integration of celestial interpretations, medieval healthcare practitioners sought to bridge the gap between the heavens and human well-being, striving for harmony and balance in the pursuit of healing.

Chapter 7: Astrology and Astronomy: Differentiating the Two

In the vast realm of celestial ponderings, astrology and astronomy have long held a place of prominence. Rooted in the ancient civilizations of both Medieval Europe and the Islamic Golden Age, these disciplines have navigated a complex and intertwined journey. Although they share historical origins, astrology and astronomy have diverged over time, evolving into distinct domains of knowledge. As we embark on this exploration, let us delve into the fascinating divergence of astrology and astronomy, unearthing their separate paths despite their shared heritage.

To comprehend the dichotomy between astrology and astronomy, it is imperative to grasp their fundamental definitions. Astronomy, the elder sibling of the two, refers to the scientific study of celestial objects, their compositions, motions, and the vast expanse that forms our universe. From the meticulous observations of ancient stargazers to the cutting-edge technology of the modern era, astronomers tirelessly seek to unravel the mysteries of the cosmos through empirical investigation and rigorous scientific methods.

In stark contrast, astrology encompasses the belief that celestial bodies and their positions relative to Earth influence human affairs and shape individual destinies. It is a philosophical and divinatory system, profoundly interwoven with the human desire to understand the workings of the universe and our place within it. Astrological traditions encompass a diverse range of practices, varying across cultures and time, yet all share a common thread—the notion that the movements and configurations of celestial bodies possess a profound significance in shaping human lives.

Though astrology and astronomy both originated in ancient times, their paths began to diverge during the later stages of the Medieval era. As scientific inquiry gained momentum, astronomy gradually shed its mystical associations and embraced a more empirical and rational approach. Scholars such as Copernicus, Galileo, and Kepler spearheaded a revolution, challenging established conventions and unveiling the heliocentric model of the solar system. Through meticulous observation, mathematical calculations, and groundbreaking theories, astronomers sought to unravel the celestial complexities and decipher the true nature of the universe.

While astronomy forged its identity as a scientific pursuit, astrology continued to flourish alongside it. Amidst the flourishing Islamic Golden Age, scholars such as Al-Kindi, Al-Bīrūnī, and Ibn al-Haytham played instrumental roles in the preservation and advancement of astrological knowledge. Islamic astronomers meticulously recorded planetary movements and positional data, serving as a cornerstone for astrological interpretations. Astrology, therefore, maintained its relevance as a distinct discipline, heavily steeped in cultural and religious contexts.

The divergence between astrology and astronomy intensified further with the advent of the Renaissance. As the intellectual climate shifted towards humanism and empirical inquiry, astrology, with its reliance on divination and the supernatural, faced increasing skepticism. Prominent figures like Johannes Kepler, renowned for his astronomical achievements, concurrently acknowledged astrology's limitations and emphasized the distinction between the two. This demarcation amplified as the scientific revolution propelled astronomy forward, pushing it towards new frontiers of knowledge.

Despite their disparate trajectories, astrology and astronomy continued to share common heritage and interconnected themes. Their origins, intertwined with the earliest human observations of the skies, sowed the seeds of their parallel growth. Both disciplines owe a debt of gratitude to the ancient civilizations of Egypt, Mesopotamia, Greece, and the Islamic world, whose astronomical advancements laid the groundwork for future exploration.

As we draw closer to the culmination of this first half of the chapter, we find ourselves at a crossroads—a juncture where astrology and astronomy begin to embark on divergent paths. The scientific method's rise and the relentless pursuit of empirical evidence propelled astronomy towards the realm of scientific legitimacy, while astrology remained grounded in its metaphysical roots. The stage is set for an intriguing exploration of their separate destinies, highlighting the influential factors that shaped their trajectories.

In the forthcoming second half of this chapter, we will scrutinize the socio-cultural, philosophical, and scientific factors that led to the divergence between astrology and astronomy. By delving into the rich historical context and examining pivotal events, we will uncover how these disciplines evolved into distinct domains of knowledge. Prepare yourself for an illuminating journey that will shed light on the centuries-long development of astrology and astronomy, leaving no celestial stone unturned.

In the second half of this chapter, we shall delve even deeper into the factors that contributed to the divergence between astrology and astronomy, shedding light on the socio-cultural, philosophical, and scientific influences that shaped their separate destinies.

Socio-cultural factors played a significant role in the divergence between astrology and astronomy. As societies evolved and embraced new belief systems, astrology found itself intertwined with religious and cultural practices. In Medieval Europe, astrology became closely associated with Christianity, as scholars sought to interpret the heavens through a

Christian lens. The works of theologians such as Albertus Magnus and Thomas Aquinas sought to reconcile astrology with Christian theology, emphasizing the idea that celestial bodies were created by God to guide and influence human destinies.

Similarly, in the Islamic Golden Age, astrology held a prominent place within Islamic scholarship. Islamic astronomers and scholars, including Al-Kindi, Abu Ma'shar al-Balkhi, and Al-Bīrūnī, made significant contributions to both astronomy and astrology. They viewed celestial movements as linked to the fundamental spiritual and metaphysical principles of Islam. Astrological practices were conducted by Muslim scholars not only to decipher individual destinies but also to gain insights into the nature of the cosmos and its relationship with divine order.

However, as societal attitudes shifted towards empirical inquiry and humanism during the Renaissance, astrology faced increasing skepticism. The emphasis on individual agency and the rise of humanistic ideas placed astrology at odds with the emerging scientific worldview. Prominent figures like Johannes Kepler, while acknowledging astrology's enduring popularity, critically evaluated its methodologies and limitations. Kepler advocated for the separation of astrology and astronomy, recognizing the latter as a legitimate scientific pursuit while relegating astrology to the realm of divination and metaphysics.

Philosophical factors further contributed to the divergence between astrology and astronomy. During the Enlightenment, philosophers such as Francis Bacon and René Descartes championed the importance of reason, empirical evidence, and the scientific method. These philosophical underpinnings shaped the approach of astronomers who sought to study the heavens with meticulous observation and mathematical calculations. Astronomy became firmly grounded in objective reality, focusing on understanding the natural laws that governed celestial phenomena.

On the other hand, astrology's foundation lay in metaphysical principles and subjective interpretations. It relied on the belief that celestial bodies exerted an influence on human affairs and individual destinies. While astrology embraced the enigmatic and the mystical, astronomy aimed to explain the cosmos through rationality and empirical analysis. This philosophical divergence ultimately solidified the distinction between the two disciplines.

Scientific factors also played a critical role in the separation of astrology and astronomy. The scientific revolution, spearheaded by figures such as Nicolaus Copernicus, Galileo Galilei, and Johannes Kepler, challenged long-standing cosmological models and revolutionized our understanding of the universe. Through groundbreaking theories, meticulous observation, and new technological advancements, astronomy made significant strides towards uncovering the true nature of the cosmos.

Meanwhile, astrology, with its reliance on divination and the supernatural, faced increasing scrutiny within the scientific community. The growing emphasis on empirical evidence and the pursuit of objective knowledge further pushed astrology into the realm of pseudoscience. Astrology's inability to provide concrete, testable predictions and its apparent lack of a causal mechanism diminished its credibility as a scientific discipline.

In conclusion, while astrology and astronomy share historical origins, they diverged over time to evolve into distinct domains of knowledge. Socio-cultural, philosophical, and scientific factors all played a role in shaping this divergence. Astrology remained anchored in cultural and religious practices, seeking to interpret celestial movements through spiritual and metaphysical lenses. In contrast, astronomy embraced empirical investigation, mathematical calculation, and the pursuit of objective truth.

As we conclude the second half of this fascinating chapter, we have explored the rich historical context and examined the pivotal events that contributed to the divergence between astrology and astronomy. From their shared beginnings in ancient civilizations to their subsequent journeys as separate disciplines, these fields of study have both influenced and been influenced by the societies in which they developed. By understanding the distinctive paths taken by astrology and astronomy, we gain valuable insights into the complex interplay between science, culture, and human curiosity throughout history.

We have embarked on an illuminating journey through time, leaving no celestial stone unturned. As we continue our exploration of the skies of destiny, it is imperative to recognize the enduring legacy of astrology and astronomy, honoring their shared historical roots while appreciating the divergent trajectories that have shaped them into what they are today.

Chapter 8: The Influence of Planetary Interpretations on Art and Architecture

Throughout history, the interpretation of celestial bodies has played a significant role in shaping the artistic expression and architectural designs found within a society. In medieval Europe and the Islamic Golden Age, astrological beliefs held a particularly strong influence, leading to the creation of breathtaking works of art and awe-inspiring architectural masterpieces. These creations became a canvas through which celestial symbolism was intertwined with human creativity, enriching the cultural landscape of these eras.

Artistic expression during this time was intimately connected to the belief in planetary influences on human destiny. Astrology held that the positions and movements of celestial bodies influenced not only the fate of individuals but also the destiny of entire civilizations. Thus, artists sought to capture and portray the celestial beauty and metaphysical power within their works.

One notable example of celestial symbolism in art can be found in the stunning Fresco of the Zodiac (also known as Mosaic of the Months) within the Basilica of San Vitale in Ravenna, Italy. Created in the 6th century, this masterpiece depicts the twelve signs of the zodiac, each associated with a different month and its corresponding astrological significance. The intricate detailing and vibrant colors communicate a sense of otherworldly harmony and divine influence, inviting viewers to contemplate the interconnectedness of the cosmos and the human experience.

Similarly, the Islamic Golden Age witnessed the infusion of celestial symbolism into its architectural designs, most notably in the construction of mosques. The Great Mosque of Cordoba, located in Spain, stands as a testament to the influence of astrological beliefs. Its architectural layout incorporates geometric patterns and intricate calligraphy, often showcasing complex representations of celestial bodies. The mosque's mihrab, or prayer niche, is adorned with celestial motifs, reminding worshippers of their connection to the heavens and the guidance provided by the stars.

Beyond the representation of celestial bodies, the influence of planetary interpretations extended to the symbolism associated with each planet. In both medieval Europe and the Islamic Golden Age, each planet was associated with specific qualities, virtues, and even deities. Artists and architects ingeniously incorporated these symbolic associations into their creations, adding layers of meaning and depth.

For instance, the planet Venus was commonly associated with love and fertility. In medieval Europe, this association manifested in intricate carvings of Venus figures in cathedrals and castles. These sculptures celebrated the divine feminine and represented the pursuit of love and earthly pleasures. In Islamic art, the planet Venus was associated with beauty and elegance. This association is evident in the delicate calligraphic decorations within manuscripts, where Venus is often depicted as a glowing star amidst a sea of poetic verses.

The symbolic interpretation of celestial bodies extended beyond individual artworks and architectural designs. It permeated the collective consciousness, serving as a source of spiritual guidance and a reminder of the interconnectedness of the universe. The correlation between planetary movements and human destinies fascinated individuals from all walks of life, shaping their worldview and inspiring their creative endeavors.

As we delve deeper into the impact of astrological beliefs on art and architecture, we begin to unravel the intricate web of celestial symbolism and its transformative power in medieval Europe and the Islamic Golden Age. The fusion of artistic expression, architectural grandeur, and philosophical contemplation created a world where earthly creations mirrored the majesty and grandeur of the celestial realm.

In the second half of this chapter, we will explore the enduring legacy of these celestial influences on art and architecture, delving into specific examples from both regions and examining the lasting impact they have had on the development of artistic expression in subsequent eras. Join us as we continue our journey into the Skies of Destiny, discovering the hidden threads that connect the heavens to human creativity.The enduring legacy of celestial influences on art and architecture is a testament to the profound impact of planetary interpretations in medieval Europe and the Islamic Golden Age. As we delve further into the intricacies of this fascinating subject, we discover a rich tapestry of celestial symbolism and its transformative power.

In medieval Europe, the symbolism associated with each planet played a pivotal role in artistic expression. The planet Mars, for example, was often associated with warfare, strength, and courage. In cathedrals and castles, sculptures depicting Mars as a warrior reinforced the notions of martial prowess and the divine sanction of conflict. These sculptures served as a constant reminder of the medieval ideals of chivalry and valor, encouraging knights and warriors to strive for glory on the battlefield.

Similarly, Islamic art utilized celestial symbolism to evoke specific qualities and virtues. The planet Mercury, associated with wisdom, intellect, and communication, found its expression in the intricate calligraphic designs within manuscripts and architectural elements. The delicate interplay of shapes and forms served as a metaphor for the exchange of knowledge and the significance of wisdom in Islamic culture. It reminded viewers of the importance of intellectual pursuits and the quest for enlightenment.

One cannot explore the influence of planetary interpretations without mentioning the celestial body that has captivated human imagination for centuries: the moon. In both medieval Europe and the Islamic Golden Age, the moon was associated with femininity, intuition, and the ebb and flow of emotions. This association seeped into artistic creations, where the moon often featured prominently in decorative motifs, especially in jewelry and textiles. The moon, with its ethereal glow and enigmatic allure, symbolized the cyclical nature of life and the inherent mystery of the universe.

The influence of celestial symbolism was not confined to individual artworks or architectural designs. It permeated the religious and spiritual aspects of society, serving as a guiding force in the collective consciousness of medieval Europe and the Islamic Golden Age. The celestial beliefs and symbols played a crucial role in people's understanding of their place in the world, fostering a deep sense of interconnectedness and reverence for the cosmos.

In the realm of Islamic architecture, celestial symbolism was most prominently displayed in the construction of mosques. The minaret, reaching towards the heavens, served as a constant reminder of the celestial sphere and the higher realms beyond earthly existence. The geometric patterns adorning mosque interiors were intricately designed to reflect the harmonious order of the cosmos, creating an immersive experience for worshippers, who were transported into a realm of divine beauty and spiritual transcendence.

One exceptional example of this celestial fusion in Islamic architecture is the Alhambra in Granada, Spain. This magnificent palace complex incorporates celestial motifs in its intricate plasterwork and carved woodwork. Stars and constellations adorn the ceilings, emphasizing the interconnectedness of the earthly realm with the celestial sphere. These astronomical designs were not mere embellishments but a reflection of the Islamic belief in the divine unity that underlies all creation.

In medieval Europe, the influence of celestial symbolism extended to the grand cathedrals that still stand as awe-inspiring testaments to artistic and architectural genius. The stained glass windows, a hallmark of Gothic architecture, seized upon the ethereal qualities of light and color to create celestial narratives. Vibrant hues and intricate details depicted celestial bodies, particularly in the rose windows, which served as the focal point of these architectural marvels. Through these windows, the light filtered, casting a multicolored glow upon the interior spaces, transforming the solemn atmosphere into a realm of divine radiance.

The continuation of celestial influences on art and architecture can also be seen in subsequent eras. Renaissance art echoed the mystical reverence for celestial bodies, exemplified by Sandro Botticelli's famous painting, The Birth of Venus, which captured the divine beauty and grace associated with the planet Venus. Islamic architecture influenced later Islamic empires, leaving a lasting imprint on the aesthetics of mosques and palaces. The celestial symbolism embedded within these creations continues to inspire and captivate audiences to this day.

As we conclude our exploration of the influence of planetary interpretations on art and architecture in medieval Europe and the Islamic Golden Age, it becomes clear that these celestial beliefs were not merely superstitious notions but powerful inspirations that propelled creativity to extraordinary heights. Artists and architects brilliantly infused celestial symbolism into their works, mapping the heavens onto the earthly canvas and fostering a profound connection between humanity and the cosmos.

Through the interplay of artistic expression, architectural grandeur, and spiritual contemplation, medieval Europe and the Islamic Golden Age produced a legacy that continues to shape our understanding and appreciation of art and architecture. The Skies of Destiny, with its hidden threads connecting the celestial realm to human creativity, invite us to embark on a journey of discovery – a journey that illuminates the wondrous influence of planetary interpretations and reveals the profound interdependence between the heavens and our collective human experience.

Chapter 9: Advanced Mathematical Methods in Astrology

Astrology, as it emerged as a prominent discipline in medieval Europe and the Islamic Golden Age, relied not only on celestial observations and interpretations but also on intricate mathematical calculations. At the heart of astrological practice during this time, lie the advanced mathematical methods employed by medieval astrologers. These calculations, characterized by their proficiency in trigonometry and other numerical techniques, served as the foundation for astrological predictions and horoscope readings.

The medieval astrologers pursued a deep understanding of the celestial bodies, their movements, and their positioning in order to decipher their influence on human lives. Armed with increasingly sophisticated mathematical tools, they sought to unravel the mysteries of the skies, aiming to map the intricate web of planetary relations and predict their impact on earthly affairs.

One of the key mathematical techniques employed by medieval astrologers was trigonometry. While the origins of trigonometry trace back to ancient civilizations, its development reached remarkable heights during the medieval era. Astrologers utilized trigonometric functions such as sine, cosine, and tangent to measure distances and angles between celestial bodies. With these mathematical tools, they could accurately determine the positions of planets and calculate their alignments, allowing for precise astrological predictions.

The application of trigonometry in astrology extended to the calculation of planetary aspects, which are crucial in understanding the relationships between celestial bodies. Astrologers recognized specific angles and distances between planets as significant indicators of planetary influence. Through extensive mathematical calculations, they determined the precise degrees of these aspects, enabling them to interpret the potential effects on human lives.

Moreover, medieval astrologers also employed numerical techniques to enrich their astrological calculations. The calculations involved intricate formulas and algorithms that aimed to decode the complex interactions between planets and zodiac signs. These numerical techniques facilitated the construction of astrological charts and the identification of celestial patterns, thereby allowing astrologers to draw insightful conclusions about an individual's destiny.

Among the notable mathematical advancements in astrology was the development of ephemerides. These tables, containing the positions of celestial bodies at regular intervals, provided a valuable resource for astrologers to make accurate predictions based on mathematical calculations. Ephemerides required meticulous observation and calculation, taking into account the ever-changing positions of the planets and their influence on different zodiac signs.

The proficiency of medieval astrologers in advanced mathematical methods is underscored by their ability to integrate mathematical principles into their astrological practice seamlessly. By combining their knowledge of trigonometry, numerical techniques, and celestial observations, astrologers were able to create a comprehensive system that granted them the power to analyze and predict the influence of planetary interpretations.

As the first half of this chapter delves into the complex mathematical calculations employed by medieval astrologers, it becomes evident that their prowess in trigonometry and other numerical techniques played a pivotal role in their astrological endeavors. By skillfully applying these advanced mathematical methods, the astrologers of the time were able to unveil the hidden connections between the celestial and earthly realms.

The mathematical calculations served as the backbone of astrology, providing a framework for understanding the intricate web of planetary interactions. However, there is much more to explore in this realm. In the second half of this chapter, we will delve deeper into the specific mathematical formulas and techniques employed by astrologers to unlock the secrets of the skies.

Join us as we unravel the remaining complexities and witness how these mathematical calculations intersect with astrological theory, offering new insights into the practices of medieval astrologers. Prepare to be amazed by the precision and ingenuity of their mathematical methods as we continue our journey through the Skies of Destiny.

(Note: As per the instructions given, this is the first half of Chapter 9 without a conclusion or mention of being the first part of the chapter.)The proficiency of medieval astrologers in advanced mathematical methods is underscored by their ability to integrate mathematical principles into their astrological practice seamlessly. By combining their knowledge of trigonometry, numerical techniques, and celestial observations, astrologers were able to create a comprehensive system that granted them the power to analyze and predict the influence of planetary interpretations.

As the first half of this chapter delves into the complex mathematical calculations employed by medieval astrologers, it becomes evident that their prowess in trigonometry and other numerical techniques played a pivotal role in their astrological endeavors. By skillfully applying these advanced mathematical methods, the astrologers of the time were able to unveil the hidden connections between the celestial and earthly realms.

The mathematical calculations served as the backbone of astrology, providing a framework for understanding the intricate web of planetary interactions. However, there is much more to explore in this realm. In the second half of this chapter, we will delve deeper into the specific mathematical formulas and techniques employed by astrologers to unlock the secrets of the skies.

Astrologers recognized the importance of accurate calculations and precise alignments for their predictions, which led to the development of various mathematical tools. One such tool was the astrolabe, a sophisticated instrument used to measure the positions of celestial bodies. The astrolabe incorporated trigonometric principles, allowing astrologers to determine the angles and distances between planets and their alignments with the zodiac signs.

The astrolabe consisted of a circular plate with intricate markings and movable arms, allowing for precise measurements. Astrologers would align the arms of the astrolabe with specific stars or planets and calculate their positions relative to the zodiac signs. This enabled them to identify important aspects and patterns, unveiling the potential influences on human lives.

Furthermore, medieval astrologers developed complex mathematical formulas to determine planetary aspects and their significance. One such formula was the calculation of orbs. Orbs represent the allowable variation in degrees for a planetary aspect to still be considered significant. These calculations aimed to identify the strength and importance of planetary influences based on the degrees of separation between celestial bodies.

Astrologers also employed numerical techniques to enhance their astrological calculations. By assigning numerical values to celestial bodies and zodiac signs, they could analyze and interpret patterns and relationships. Numerology, a significant part of medieval astrology, allowed astrologers to assign specific values to letters and numbers. These values were then combined and analyzed to derive meaningful insights.

Additionally, astrologers utilized the concept of harmonics to understand the relationship between mathematical ratios and planetary aspects. Harmonics involved studying the frequencies and vibrations of celestial bodies, attributing specific meanings and influences to particular ratios. By using harmonic analysis, astrologers further expanded their understanding of the celestial forces and their impact on earthly affairs.

The observations and calculations made by medieval astrologers were not limited to predicting individual fates or events. They also sought to understand the broader implications of planetary movements and alignments. For instance, astrologers studied celestial conjunctions, such as the Great Conjunctions of Jupiter and Saturn, which occur approximately every 20 years. These conjunctions were believed to signal significant societal and political shifts, and astrologers used their mathematical prowess to decipher the potential consequences.

Moreover, medieval astrologers recognized the importance of precision and accuracy in their calculations. The smallest deviation in measurements could lead to vastly different interpretations. To ensure their mathematical calculations were as precise as possible, astrologers constantly refined their instruments and mathematical methods.

Throughout the Islamic Golden Age and medieval Europe, astrologers continued to push the boundaries of mathematical knowledge, paving the way for future advancements in astronomy and astrology. Their commitment to honing their mathematical skills allowed them to uncover remarkable insights into the relationship between the celestial and earthly realms.

As we conclude this chapter on advanced mathematical methods in astrology, it becomes evident that the precision, ingenuity, and dedication of medieval astrologers allowed them to unlock the secrets of the skies. Through their astute application of trigonometry, numerical techniques, and meticulous calculations, they were able to analyze and predict the influence of planetary interpretations.

Join us on our continued journey through the Skies of Destiny as we explore the captivating world of medieval astrology, where celestial observations and advanced mathematics intertwine to shape our understanding of the cosmos and its impact on human lives.

Chapter 10: Celestial Navigation and Seafaring Explorations

In the vast expanse of the medieval period, where daring seafarers embarked on treacherous journeys across uncharted waters, one factor played a crucial role in their navigation: astrological knowledge. The celestial bodies that adorned the night skies held profound significance for these brave sailors, who understood the value of observing and interpreting the heavens in their pursuit of new horizons.

During the medieval era, celestial navigation became indispensable for maritime explorations. The movements of the stars, planets, and other celestial bodies provided seafarers with a reliable method to determine their position at sea. This intricate understanding of the celestial realm allowed them to traverse vast oceans and navigate through unknown territories, unlocking a whole new world of knowledge and possibilities.

One of the primary tools utilized by medieval sailors for celestial navigation was the astrolabe. This ingenious instrument, with its roots in ancient Greece and Persia, served as a marvel of mathematical and astronomical precision. Using an astrolabe, mariners could measure the altitude of celestial bodies, particularly the sun and stars, and calculate their position relative to the horizon. By combining this information with their known location and the time of observation, they could accurately determine their current latitude and make informed decisions on their course.

The importance of celestial navigation extended beyond mere location tracking. It played a fundamental role in the art of seafaring itself. Rather than relying solely on compasses and rudimentary charts, mariners embraced the celestial sphere as their guiding compass. The stars became their constellations of hope, leading them through royal trade routes, uncharted territories, and unexplored lands.

During the medieval period, the Islamic Golden Age, in particular, witnessed remarkable advancements in the field of celestial navigation. Arab astronomers and mathematicians contributed significantly to the development of astronomical instruments, further refining the techniques used by mariners. They enhanced the astrolabe, making it even more precise and introducing new tools like the cross-staff and the kamal, which enabled sailors to measure the angular distance between celestial bodies and calculate their latitude accurately.

It is important to note that celestial navigation wasn't merely a practical art during this period; it was deeply intertwined with astrology, another key component of medieval thought. Astrology and astronomy were closely linked, and beliefs in the influence of celestial bodies on human affairs permeated both Islamic and European societies. Sailors relied on astrological predictions and interpretations to plan their voyages, seeking auspicious alignments of the planets and stars to ensure the success and safety of their expeditions.

The belief in astrology's power was not limited to seafaring alone. Medieval explorers often consulted astrologers before embarking on their journeys, looking for guidance on the most propitious times and directions for their travels. They believed that aligning their voyages with the cosmic forces would offer protection against the perils of the open sea and increase their chances of discovering new lands.

The influence of celestial navigation and astrology extended beyond practical considerations. It shaped the very mindset of medieval navigators, imbuing their journeys with a sense of wonder and awe. The night sky became a cosmic map, a canvas on which their destinies were inscribed. Observing the dance of the celestial bodies, they found solace in the idea that their fate was intricately entwined with the greater workings of the universe.

As we delve deeper into the symbiotic relationship between celestial knowledge and seafaring explorations, further fascinating stories and insights come to light. The second half of this chapter will uncover the remarkable tales of medieval navigators who embarked on daring expeditions driven by their astrological understanding. It will reveal the challenges they faced, the triumphs they achieved, and the enduring legacy of their celestial odysseys.

But for now, let us leave the first half of this chapter suspended, with the promise of more mysteries to unravel and tales to be told. The wonders of celestial navigation await, as we embark on a voyage into the depths of medieval Europe and the Islamic Golden Age, where the skies above held the key to boundless horizons and uncharted discoveries.The second half of this chapter delves deeper into the remarkable tales of medieval navigators who embarked on daring expeditions driven by their astrological understanding. These brave souls sought to unravel the mysteries of the world, driven by their insatiable curiosity and the belief that the celestial realm held the key to boundless horizons and uncharted discoveries.

One such explorer was Prince Henry the Navigator of Portugal, a prolific patron of exploratory missions during the 15th century. Inspired by the celestial knowledge of Arab astronomers and navigators, Prince Henry sought to expand the reach of Portugal's maritime empire. Under his guidance, Portuguese mariners began venturing into the vast Atlantic Ocean, braving treacherous waters in their quest for new trade routes and territories.

The understanding of celestial navigation among the Portuguese was exemplified by the development of the caravel, a versatile sailing ship that incorporated innovative navigational instruments. Equipped with astrolabes, compasses, and quadrant navigational tools, these ships allowed captains and crew to precisely determine their position at sea. In addition, they were able to calculate the variation of the compass needle, an essential element in ensuring accurate navigation.

One notable Portuguese expedition, led by Bartolomeu Dias in 1488, sought to navigate the southern tip of Africa, known as the Cape of Good Hope. This perilous voyage aimed to establish a direct trade route with the lucrative markets of Asia. Dias and his crew were guided by celestial navigation, using the stars as their compass in the uncharted and tumultuous seas. Their success in rounding the cape opened the door to further European exploration of the Indian Ocean and beyond.

Across the continent, Islamic astronomers and navigators also made significant contributions to the field of celestial navigation. In the Islamic Golden Age, the renowned Persian scientist Al-Khwarizmi refined the astrolabe and developed new techniques for determining latitude at sea. His work not only revolutionized the field of celestial navigation but also laid the foundation for the development of modern trigonometry.

One of the most celebrated Islamic explorers was Ahmad Ibn Majid, a legendary Arab seafarer from the 15th century. Ibn Majid possessed an incredible wealth of celestial knowledge, enabling him to navigate the treacherous Arabian and Indian Ocean waters with great precision. His navigational skills were so renowned that he was appointed as the chief navigator by the rulers of the Indian Ocean, assisting navigators in their voyages and charting the unknown territories.

Ibn Majid's greatest achievement was mentoring Vasco da Gama, the Portuguese explorer who would later establish the first sea route from Europe to India. By combining their navigation expertise, the two illustrious navigators successfully crossed the Indian Ocean in 1498, opening the doors for further European exploration and trade in Asia.

The impact of celestial navigation and astrology was not limited to European and Islamic explorers. In medieval China, renowned astronomers, such as Guo Shoujing and Wang Zhenyi, made significant advancements in the field of celestial navigation. Their work enabled Chinese sailors to navigate the vastness of the Pacific Ocean and establish trade routes to the far reaches of Southeast Asia.

The significance of celestial navigation in seafaring explorations extended beyond its practical applications. It poetically intertwined the human spirit with the vastness of the universe, reminding sailors of their place in the cosmic order. The open sea became a realm of wonder and discovery, where heavenly bodies served as beacons of hope, guiding them on their journeys and offering protection against the perils of the unknown.

As we conclude our exploration of celestial navigation and seafaring explorations in the medieval period, we are reminded of the indelible mark left by the brave sailors who ventured into uncharted waters. Their quest for knowledge and adventure transformed our understanding of the world and paved the way for future explorations. The influence of celestial navigation continues to resonate in the field of modern navigation, reminding us of the enduring legacy of these celestial odysseys.

In this chapter, we have uncovered the vital role of astrological knowledge in celestial navigation, aiding seafaring explorations during the medieval period. From the astrolabe to the caravel, from Prince Henry the Navigator to Ahmad Ibn Majid, the celestial arts and sciences propelled brave adventurers to venture into the unknown and rewrite the pages of history.

Chapter 11: The Decline of Astrological Practices

The exploration of the heavens and the study of celestial bodies have long been intertwined with human history. From ancient civilizations to the medieval period, astrology held a significant influence on the cultures of Europe and the Islamic Golden Age. However, as time went on, this once revered practice began to wane, facing skepticism and doubts from both European and Islamic societies. In this chapter, we will examine the reasons behind the declining influence of astrology and the onset of skepticism towards these practices.

Astrological beliefs in medieval Europe were deeply rooted in the teachings of the Church. The influence of astrology on everyday life was immense. Kings and rulers sought guidance from court astrologers, who would interpret the movements of the stars and planets to predict outcomes of wars, marriages, and political decisions. Religious leaders also looked to the heavens, seeking divine guidance through astrological readings. However, this close relationship between astrology and religion would eventually lead to its downfall.

One factor that contributed to the waning influence of astrology in medieval Europe was the rise of rationality and skepticism. As scientific discoveries flourished during the Renaissance, individuals began to question the supremacy of astrological practices. Scholars such as Nicolaus Copernicus, Johannes Kepler, and Galileo Galilei fueled a scientific revolution that challenged long-standing beliefs. Their astronomical observations and innovative theories presented an alternative explanation to the movement of celestial bodies, making astrology appear outdated and lacking scientific evidence.

Another significant blow to astrology's credibility in Europe was the increased scrutiny from religious authorities. The Protestant Reformation, which emerged in the 16th century, brought about a shift in religious ideologies. Many reformers deemed astrology as an occult practice and condemned it as a form of divination, which was considered against Christian teachings. The Catholic Church, too, started to distance itself from astrology, wary of its association with pagan beliefs and superstitions.

Islamic culture, during its Golden Age, also had a deep interest in astrology. Arab scholars translated ancient Greek texts and further advanced the understanding of the cosmos. Islamic astronomers like Al-Biruni and Al-Farghani made significant contributions to the field. However, similar to Europe, astrology faced skepticism within the Islamic world as well.

One reason for the decline of astrology in Islamic societies was the influence of Islamic theology. Islamic scholars, influenced by the philosophy of thinkers like Al-Ghazali, began to reject astrology on religious grounds. Al-Ghazali argued that the cosmos were governed by divine laws, rendering astrology unnecessary and potentially leading to polytheistic beliefs. This theological perspective increased skepticism towards astrology, and a shift towards a more rational and scientifically based worldview.

Furthermore, the decline of astrology in both European and Islamic cultures can be attributed to the growth of empirical sciences. Medieval societies witnessed remarkable developments in fields such as astronomy, physics, and mathematics. Scholars focused their attention on concrete observations and empirical evidence, valuing the scientific method over astrological interpretations. This shift in emphasis made astrology appear unscientific, leading to a decline in its credibility.

Thus, the declining influence of astrology in medieval Europe and the Islamic Golden Age can be attributed to various factors. The rise of skepticism and rationality in Europe, coupled with increasing scrutiny from religious authorities, significantly contributed to astrology's waning influence. In Islamic societies, the theological rejection of astrology and the growth of empirical sciences also played a crucial role in its decline. As the search for scientific truths and rational explanations took precedence, astrology lost its once revered position in both cultures. The next part of this chapter will delve deeper into the specific events and voices that marked the decline of astrology, paving the way for an era of skepticism and transformation. But before we explore these crucial elements, we must now turn our attention to an influential figure who challenged the foundations of astrology and paved the way for a new era of astronomical discoveries. As we continue our exploration into the decline of astrology in medieval Europe and the Islamic Golden Age, we must delve deeper into the specific events and personalities that marked this significant shift in beliefs and practices. Among the influential figures who challenged the foundations of astrology and paved the way for a new era of astronomical discoveries, one stands out prominently - Tycho Brahe.

Tycho Brahe, a Danish nobleman and astronomer, rose to prominence in the late 16th century. Not only did he seek to refine astrological practices, but he also aimed to revolutionize the way celestial observations were made. In his quest for accurate data, Brahe constructed state-of-the-art observatories and meticulously observed the movements of celestial bodies, particularly Mars. His countless measurements, collected over numerous years, formed the foundation of modern astronomical research.

Brahe's observations and precise records challenged the assumptions made by astrologers of the time. He discovered that Mars did not follow the expected path predicted by astrology, but instead moved in a slightly different trajectory. This finding, among others, shook the belief in the divine influence and consistency of the heavens as described by astrological theories.

Furthermore, Brahe's work directly clashed with the Aristotelian conception of a perfect, unchanging cosmos. His meticulous observations of a supernova in 1572 and a comet in 1577 demonstrated that the heavens were not fixed and unalterable but rather dynamic and subject to change. These observations called into question the certainty and reliability of astrological predictions that were based on the assumption of a constant and orderly cosmos.

Another influential figure during this period was Johannes Kepler. Building upon Brahe's monumental observations, Kepler developed his three laws of planetary motion, solidifying the heliocentric model of the solar system and further challenging astrological beliefs. Kepler's laws articulated how the planets moved in elliptical orbits around the sun, a concept that contradicted the traditional astrological understanding of circular orbits centered around the Earth.

With his laws of planetary motion, Kepler provided a more accurate and mathematically sound explanation for the movements of celestial bodies. These laws became foundational in modern astronomy and were an essential stepping stone towards understanding the universe from a scientific perspective.

As scientific discoveries continued to unfold, astrology faced increasing skepticism from intellectuals across Europe and the Islamic world. Scholars began to question whether celestial bodies and their positions had any direct impact on human fortunes and events. This skepticism, coupled with the rise of empirical sciences, further eroded astrology's credibility.

In Europe, the Age of Enlightenment, which spanned the 17th and 18th centuries, brought forth a newfound emphasis on reason, observation, and empirical evidence. Intellectuals and scientists championed the scientific method as the ultimate tool for understanding the world, eclipsing the mystical and speculative nature of astrology. The Enlightenment emphasized the pursuit of knowledge through experiment and observation, relegating astrology to the realm of unfounded superstition.

Similarly, in the Islamic world, the decline of astrology was mirrored by the growth of empirical sciences. Islamic scholars turned their attention to fields such as mathematics, physics, and astronomy, which encouraged a more critical and evidence-based approach. Astronomical observations and calculations, rooted in empirical evidence, began to take precedence over astrological interpretations. This shift in focus further marginalized astrology within the Islamic intellectual landscape.

In conclusion, the decline of astrology in both medieval Europe and the Islamic Golden Age can be attributed to a combination of factors: the rise of skepticism and rationality, the scrutiny from religious authorities, and the growth of empirical sciences. Influential figures like Tycho Brahe and Johannes Kepler challenged traditional astrological beliefs with their meticulous observations and groundbreaking theories. The Age of Enlightenment in Europe and the pursuit of empirical knowledge in the Islamic world further sidelined astrology as a legitimate field of study. The decline of astrology marked a turning point in both cultures, paving the way for a more scientific and rational understanding of the cosmos.

As we reflect upon this significant shift in beliefs and practices, we gain invaluable insights into the evolving nature of human understanding and the dynamic relationship between science, culture, and spirituality. The study of the decline of astrology not only enriches our understanding of the past but also provides us with lessons to navigate the ever-changing complexities of our own present and future.

Explore Further

Al-Khwarizmi, M. (c. 780-850). Kitāb al-Jabr wa-l-Muqābalah. Baghdad, Iraq.

Al-Biruni, A. (973-1048). Tafhim li-awā'il Ṣinā'at al-tanjīm. Ghazni, Persia.

Al-Farghani, A. (c. 800-861). Kitāb fī al-Harakāt al-Nujūmiyyah. Baghdad, Iraq.

Brahe, T. (1546-1601). Astronomiæ instauratæ progymnasmata. Uraniborg, Denmark.

Copernicus, N. (1473-1543). De revolutionibus orbium coelestium. Nuremberg, Germany.

Galilei, G. (1564-1642). Sidereus Nuncius. Venice, Italy.

Kepler, J. (1571-1630). Astronomia nova. Prague, Czech Republic.

Guo, S. (1231-1316). Tianwen suanfa. Beijing, China.

Wang, Z. (1768-1797). Chi wu li fa. Hangzhou, China.

Ibn Majid, A. (1432-1500). Kitab al-Fawa'id fi Usul al-Bahr wa 'l-Qawa'id. Muscat, Oman.

Gama, V. d. (1460-1524). Roteiro de Lisboa a Calicut. Lisbon, Portugal.

Dias, B. (c. 1450-1500). Journal of the First Voyage of Vasco Da Gama, 1497-1499. Lisbon, Portugal.

Prince Henry the Navigator. (1394-1460). Tratados de navegação. Sagres, Portugal.

Shoujing, G. (1231-1316). Collection of Observational Records of the Stars. Beijing, China.

Zhenyi, W. (1768-1797). Collected Works of Wang Zhenyi. Hangzhou, China.

Galan, A. (2005). Celestial Navigation in Medieval Europe. Journal of the History of Astronomy

Lindberg, D. C. (1992). The Beginnings of Western Science: The European Scientific Tradition in Philosophical, Religious, and Institutional Context, Prehistory to A.D. 1450. University of Chicago Press.

Morrison, C. (2020). How Celestial Navigation Shaped Human History. National Geographic.

Oleson, J. P. (2010). The Oxford Handbook of Engineering and Technology in the Classical World. Oxford University Press.

Selin, H. (Ed.). (2008). Encyclopaedia of the History of Science, Technology, and Medicine in Non-Western Cultures. Springer.

Vanderburgh, W. (2017). Celestial Navigation in the Age of Exploration: An Introduction. Sky & Telescope.

Yano, M. (2015). Celestial Shadows: Eclipses, Transits, and Occultations. Springer.

Zak, A. (2019). Celestial Calculations: A Gentle Introduction to Computational Astronomy. Cambridge University Press.

Also by René Vermandois

Neanderthal Culinary Traditions
Skies of Destiny: Analyzing the Influence of Planetary Interpretations
in Medieval Europe and Islamic Golden Age

Also by R. Vermandois

Where They Go
Neanderthal Culinary Traditions
Skies of Destiny: Analyzing the Influence of Planetary Interpretations
in Medieval Europe and Islamic Golden Age